GJERTRUD SCHNACKENBERG

The Throne of Labdacus

GJERTRUD SCHNACKENBERG was born in 1953. Her many awards include fellowships from the Guggenheim Foundation and the National Endowment for the Arts, the Rome Prize in Literature, and an Award in Literature from the American Academy of Arts and Letters.

ALSO BY GJERTRUD SCHNACKENBERG

Portraits and Elegies (1982)

The Lamplit Answer (1985)

A Gilded Lapse of Time (1992)

Supernatural Love: Poems 1976–1992 (2000)

THE THRONE
OF LABDACUS

THE THRONE
OF LABDACUS

GJERTRUD
SCHNACKENBERG

Farrar, Straus and Giroux

NEW YORK

FARRAR, STRAUS AND GIROUX
19 Union Square West, New York 10003

Distributed in Canada by Douglas & McIntyre Ltd.
Printed in the United States of America
Published in 2000 by Farrar, Straus and Giroux
First paperback edition, 2001

Grateful acknowledgment is made to the Getty Research Institute for the History
of Art and the Humanities, which commissioned a part of "The God Tunes the
Strings."

Library of Congress Cataloging-in-Publication Data
Schnackenberg, Gjertrud.
      The throne of Labdacus / Gjertrud Schnackenberg.— 1st ed.
         p. cm.
      ISBN 0-374-52796-2 (pbk).
         1. Oedipus (Greek mythology)—Poetry. 2. Apollo (Greek deity)—
Poetry. 3. Mythology, Greek—Poetry. I. Title.

PS3569.C5178 T48 2000
811'.54—dc21
                                                              00-028416

Designed by Gretchen Achilles

TO ROBERT

Every day, my salvation

ONE

✦

THE GOD
TUNES THE
STRINGS

The first warning passing through Thebes—
As small a sound

As a housefly alighting from Persia
And stamping its foot on a mound

Where the palace once was;
As small as a moth chewing thread

In the tyrant's robe;
As small as the cresting of red

In the rim of an injured eye; as small
As the sound of a human conceived—

The god in Delphi,
Mouthing the words;

Then the god begins tuning the strings
With the squeak of the wooden pegs

Rotating in their holes,
As if he were setting the tragic text

To the music of houseflies.
A resinous *skreak* being dragged

Through too-small peg holes,
A sound that signifies

The god's unwillingness to speak;
Recalcitrance; unease the god can't quell

At the first oracle: *Flee from birth.* At which a string
Shudders inaudibly, a premonition

That even the god will be frightened, leaning above
The premiere of *Oedipus*,

The god frightened
By the self-blinding—and a story,

The meaning of which nobody knows,
Or whose meaning *is* that nobody knows,

Though once upon a time
The god of poetry

Told the whole story of Oedipus
In one flashing sentence,

In the time it takes for the heart to beat once—
The prophecy he gave to Oedipus

While Oedipus gazed at the god
With uninjured eyes—

A story like a Sphinx-dictated riddle
Even the god can't solve,

A story sent to the god
By Faceless Necessity

Who had held a clay tablet up
To the bandaged eyes

Of a Bound Man
Playing his harp with his feet,

The most archaic tablet
Merely a copy of a still more archaic tablet,

The long-broken, unrecoverable original
First sent to him, the earliest tablet

With a story about a nameless foundling
Lost on the mountainside of his own life,

Written, not in Greek, but in the language
Of the gods,

In gouged-out marks like howls of laughter
And brief, snuffed screams,

Tablets homely, sunken, heavy,
Lightless, pockmarked,

Like pieces broken from the moon
Above the citadel of Thebes—

A story scourging the mud surface like a plague,
A Mycenaean folktale told

In a whispering poetry,
Something about the woman's cleft,

And a hint that Thebes, secretly wounded,
Secretly bled,

And a childbirth bed in an ancient palace
And an infant maimed and left for dead,

An orphan king abandoned on a mountain,
A mountain we can visit to this day,

And from the start the story had
The god's name fastened like a worm

To its heart the way the worm appears
Out of nowhere and fastens itself

To the mortal ones, with a message
Unintelligible beyond itself.

Simply a *making known*—
Making known *what is*.

What is: a leaking-through of events
From beyond the bourn of right and wrong;

What is: a sequence of accidents
Without a cause,

Or from which the cause
Is long-lost, like a ruthless jewel

Missing from an archaic setting's
Empty, bent, but still aggressive prongs.

Some said they heard the pegs squeaking in the holes
Of the lyre as if the god were setting a text

To the music of wooden wheels
On a stridulous cart passing out of Thebes

Forever—and indeed, nothing here is hidden,
And it never was, not even long before

These Thebans were brought to birth,
And Eyeless Necessity unreeled

Her crimson thread
To dangle it before the kitten-Sphinx

Flexing her paws on the steps
Of the Theban palace, a thread

She seized and lashed with her tiny claws—
Nothing is hidden,

But whether his eyes are open or closed
The god sees

A wooden cart that has left Thebes behind
In the far, far distance: a flea-circus cart ridden

By a miles-away, miniature king,
An irritable king, impetuous, Mycenaean,

Threatening with his goad—
And coming to visit the god,

Coming to inquire about the fate
Of the three-day-old he put aside.

The unnamed one. At the sight of which
The god stops the strings' vibration

By pressing the strings with his palm,
As if he were patting the ashes

In overloaded urns, the ashes of tyrants
Packed with the dust of so many people:

This was the house of Labdacus;
These were the people of Thebes.

Laius, don't have a child. But the god
Cannot choose who is born.

Past and future tangle in his strings
Together with oracles crushed under wheels

And resin powder squeaking against wood,
Dusting the ivory and silver and carved horn

Of the lyre with the squeak
Of the pegs, like the foot of Laius on the night

He crossed Jocasta's threshold;
To this day no one knows

Whether Laius believed or disbelieved
The prophecy, or whether Laius heard

The pegs rotating in their holes in Delphi
With an oracle that someone is conceived.

To this day, no one knows
If Laius saw, or could not see,

Above the citadel of Thebes,
The shining, far above, of untouched snows.

TWO

✧

THE SHAPE OF
LIGHTNING

Oracles fulfilled long ago
And out in the open for all to see,

Yet seen by no one
But a god and a shepherd; and two masked figures

Holding the broken halves of a prophecy
Whose jagged seams they press together

And see the shape of lightning, dirtied, dark;
The oracles coming true, but in the past;

And not to fulfill a law. There is no need.
The laws are *there*, fulfilled or unfulfilled.

The god simply says,
I saw what I saw—

A throne of snow.
A threatening goad.

A digger's foot tamping down
And tamping down a mound at the place

Where three roads meet, leaving no visible evidence
Of who was buried there—

A father crossing a threshold;
A son crossing it.

With a gust of notes, in flurries
Striking the blue air, each note with a word,

In Delphi the god is overheard
Speaking as if interpreting a dream:

A foot signifies a slave,
An injured foot a failed escape—

In Thebes, the people see unfathomed sacrilege
In swiftly succeeding, savage episodes;

But in Athens, the people quarrel
Over what is meant—

For some, the god makes no demand,
Seeks no response,

And there is nothing humans have
That the god wants.

For some, the story is clotted
With punishment and bruising justice

Making its fist felt; some blame the ignorance
Of Oedipus, some blame the gods' omniscience;

For some, the tragedy unfolds without a moral—
No how or why; no spelling out of fate

Or sacrifice or punishment; merely the god's
Swift brushing-by, scented with laurel.

And for others it is only an ancient folktale
About a guiltless crime:

Not a judgment, not a warning,
Not an example, not a command—

Merely a tale in which neither the gods
Nor the human ones can claim that they meant

To harm or to save, to kill or to stay their hands.
Merely a piling-up of consequence,

With a bleeding-through of episodes and accidents.
And, all over Greece,

The unjudging rhapsodes ready themselves,
Tuning their lyres, needing no evidence.

And, from mountains-away Olympus:
Icy silence.

But whether the thing is known or unknown,
Said or unsaid, seen or unseen—

Whether the scrolls of the Oedipus text
Unroll or spring shut,

Outside the walls of a stone palace
A man is rooted to the ground,

Begging *What, what, what* as a life-and-death
Riddle is posed by a slave

And events pour toward him from his past
Like waves of sound from the god,

Swift waves—
And a human hand reaching above—

Swift, swift, wing-swiftness, so swift
Even the gods were caught up

Though whether they saw it as the work
Of a single moment, day, or life;

Whether they saw it as the work of generations
Hanging persecuted among the world-cycles,

Or as a fall that happened only once,
To one man alone; or as what happened to them all—

Even the god of poetry can't tell.
Things done blindly, things, *things*

Done on earth; human things; with a gap
Between what is done and what is seen,

What is seen and what is known,
Whereas, in the gods' reality

The same things are done, but with open eyes—
With open eyes they fasten on *what is*.

Though the housefly stalks across the gold-leaf
Eyelashes of the gods, they do not blink;

They sit enraptured in their shining chairs,
Gazing at Thebes.

THREE

☫

WHAT-IS
AND
WHAT-IS-NOT

What-is and what-is-not
Seesawed above bright Greece,

And the god fled from ice-crowned Necessity
And the hundreds of tablets

She'd sent as gifts, as threats, as messages,
As binding commands: *This story will be*

Written. And in your hand. Across tablets
Broken by the god into ankle-deep rubble,

He fled, and took a seat on a stone bench
In a dim, low-ceilinged tablet-house

A safe distance from barren Thebes,
Merely a scribe, homely-faced and shrunken,

Lyreless, and seated amid a school of scribes,
The god of poetry scribbling in Linear B,

Merely scratching out lists of supplies
Of helmets and shields for a local infantry,

And tallies of the royal chariots,
And tables for counting by fifties

The populations of cattle and sheep; then turning
To more savage reckonings,

Writing out the names of humans by the thousands,
As if humans were merely quantities

To be counted out and bundled into sheaves
And flooded with a senseless inventory

Of innumerable gods; scribbling ever faster,
As if his life's work were to record

At the last split second every human and god
Who was carried off in the catastrophe—

Then the god ceased writing, as if the Greek palaces
Had caught fire and were burning beneath the star

By which once upon a time Oedipus navigated
His way hurriedly from Delphi

Into Thebes, then stopped
To wash his father's blood off in the fountain

While outside the Theban walls the god had stalked
Back and forth, holding his lyre under his arm—

And the god's writing tablets were dumped into our age
From Homer's "black sack of trouble"—

Tablets that humans found when the pits were opened
At the foot of the palace,

With a sickening gust from the Sphinx
In the shovel pans of the diggers—

Polybus has taken the present prophecies with him
To Hades where he lies hidden—they are worthless—

Tablets that look, even in dark-age fragments,
Like former possessions of Apollo:

No poetry whispers there; no text;
Yet their aura belongs to the god,

Together with the violent diadems
Crumpled into gold geometrical objects;

And dagger hoards; and a tiny, ivory-carved chair
With an inlaid game board for a buried child;

And splinters of Near Eastern chariot wheels that revolved
Through the hinterlands of Greece,

And a length of rope
Splayed at the end and unraveled to its fossil-core

As if it had been sawn through by the horrific sawing
Of Oedipus' jeweled sword,

A rope that leads nowhere, like an orphan's family tie.
Like Jocasta's dusty cord.

And an enigmatic bone:
Ares' dark-brown jaw, still ravening.

But Eyeless Necessity's messenger
Found him, even there,

Appearing at the low door of the tablet-house,
With a basket over his arm,

Bending to enter, then approaching the god—
Recognizable by his shining feet—

A gift-bringer from Necessity's palace
With a basket of offerings to deliver

Directly into the god's hands:
Fresh, still-wet tablets, with the Oedipus tale.

The god touched the tablets like a blind man,
Then wiped with his palm

The tale of Oedipus into a smear
And substituted, on behalf of Zeus, a law

That vibrated in the heavens
With Zeus's pity:

The human being, in the end, is an injured body.
An injured body that lies where no law

Can touch it. An injured body that lies unburied
Outside the bourn of right and wrong.

But he had written this in the language of the gods:
The tablets showed only an expanse of illegible waves

Like a depiction of Zeus's rain in undulating sheets
Whipping a storm through Thebes

With the rustling of a pair of suddenly folded,
Wet Sphinx-wings; but then,

Beneath the freshly written law of Zeus,
The old story began showing through—

Once upon a time, a fate attached itself to Thebes
The way a cut attaches itself to the skin,

And it was the gods who manhandled the knife,
Clumsy, butcherous—like a Sphinx's folktale

About sawing a man to pieces to look for his soul,
And finding only blood, tissues, bones,

But no evidence of his soul, and nothing
Of the man himself—he wiped the tablet again,

And rested his powerful hand on the clay,
Letting it sink. A riddle he couldn't resolve

In poetry. But the god lifted his hand
From the sucking clay, and saw that a wordless tablet

Could depict the speechless infant
Gazing at the god from the mountainside,

A nameless baby who gazes
At a world without a name,

Things without names, space in the dark
And time without a world passing through it;

Things; *things;* things passed down
In families, like infirmities,

Like facial features fused into one's children's
Children, like the pulsing of the eyes' black pupils

Enlarging and contracting into points—
Black gems, handed down;

The nameless gaze of a nameless child
Stripping the god of speech,

Striking into the god, leaving him bereft
Of his attributes—poetry, healing, music—

Leaving the god alone on the mountainside
With a set of Necessity's tablets once again.

According to some, with one spoken hexameter the god
Burned down the palaces of the Bronze Age,

Fusing the tablets into memory's cremated
Foundations, leaving him all alone above Thebes

With white plumes drifting over Greece
Like feathers from the aviary of Tiresias;

They said it was the god's work
That brought writing to an end in Greece;

There ceased to be scribes
Attached to the palaces; the art was lost;

The story was locked up in silence,
The image of Oedipus expunged,

The phrase suppressed: *Ill-starred man,*
May you never know who you are.

But even so, in a world where nothing
Could be written and no one could read,

The story floated forward.
As if the story were telling itself.

Even so, ancient gossip swirled
Around a figure rooted next to a stone palace

Long after the people had fled the house
In the late Bronze Age, a house reviled

By every single living human being,
Including its own inhabitants,

Where Tiresias spoke as the god's mouthpiece:
Gaunt you will be, as the god mouthed the words;

Where a fly stamped its foot at a tyrant
And that tiny vibration took hold

In the Theban walls and caused
A dynastic jar to smash from a shelf

With a family's miniature portrait faces
Staring out, Laius, Jocasta, Oedipus, Antigone,

Isolated from one another, each
Abandoned on the separate mountain peaks

Of a miniature red mountain range,
An injured dynasty in terra-cotta crags.

And the tyrant who claimed the throne of Labdacus
Depicted jabbering I . . . I . . . I . . .

Holding a fragment of a broken painted jar,
The other pieces strewn at his feet

Like dried-red icicle-oracles, the meaning pouring away
And leaving the story, in jagged pieces, behind.

And the god's face depicted there as well,
Watching from the ruins

Together with the slave who admitted
He disobeyed Laius, and covered his hair with his hands—

FOUR

✾

THE
SHEPHERD
SPEAKS

From the shroud came
The gaze an infant bestows,

In untouchable, wavering, radiant waves;
Like a god's gaze, found in solitude.

An infant maimed and left for dead. I stood
In the shrinking snows. I knew the oracle.

I knew what the god had said.
I covered my eyes with my hands.

But there are things we do
Not for the sake of the gods

But for other men. I lowered my hands again
And looked: an infant left for dead.

There was no arguing backward,
No looking ahead.

At the sight of the infant's gaze
I was riveted, chosen, beguiled.

I knew what the oracle said.
And I rescued the child.

FIVE

♕

AN ORACLE
PASSES THROUGH
THEBES

Delicately, as if plucking a single fate
From a heap of entangled fates,

The god touches, with a plectrum, a single string:
Flee from birth. And watches from his blinding mountain.

Sound waves move toward Thebes. At which
The diadem of Laius darkens

As if it were already buried in soil.
As if gold were a flame that could go out.

When the god touches the string
An oracle passes through Thebes.

Too late; always too late.
Some said a warning passed along the Theban walls

Like a pitch vibrating down the length
Of a string. *Laius, don't have a child.*

Then, invisibly, the sound moved away.
Moved far off. The string was stilled.

Some said they heard only
A silence leaking from Delphi.

Some thought it was deliberately spilled.
As if the silence had been willed.

Others, that a flash flood of silence
Engulfed Thebes.

And some believed the sound was neither given
As a warning, nor interpreted as one.

But when the oracle passed through Thebes
Everyone shivered and looked up the path

To the gate that faced the mountain;
Jocasta sat up in bed with a start;

Perhaps it was crickets thrumming on the barren slopes
Like a slowly pulsing heart—

But a gravely wounded infant could starve
Or die from the cold or be eaten by wolves

Or shriek and turn blue
With his *psyche* leaking out of his wounds,

His soul escaping from his leaking eyes—
Labdacus sleeps safely in his grave

Outside the walls of the peaceful city,
Past harm; but Laius tosses in his bed

And breathes jaggedly
Like a man gazing helplessly in his dream

At the infant child he has put aside,
Abandoned, in the wilderness, on a mountain.

An inner wilderness. An inner mountain.
The god sets his lyre down on the floor

Beside his chair in Delphi,
Then steps, with a shining foot, to enter Thebes—

But the oracles are aborted, broken
Into aborted insights, revelation ever further reduced,

Strewn at the threshold; held fast, then seen
To be useless; fateless; a glinting in the dark

On a bedroom floor in Thebes, and the god stoops
In the darkened room,

Then shrinks from the bloodied jewels—far off,
A flurry of notes, a gust of archaic music blowing past

From the time when humans and deities
Played musical instruments together,

From the time when the god allowed
Versions of the legend to circulate

By word of mouth—the god's own versions,
As if he were telling and interpreting his own dream

To the citizens of Thebes, and no one could examine
What was said—gossip, folktale, rumor, dream,

Somebody heard that somebody heard
That somebody heard that such-and-such happened,

Somebody said that somebody said
That this had happened,

But no one knew to whom, or when.
And no one knew what to believe.

Some said the slave had given his own child,
Not the king's, to the childless king of Corinth;

Some said that Oedipus survived his deeds intact,
And sat, in great old age,

At his banquet table with his sons;
Some said that Oedipus did what he did with open eyes,

Continuing to reign
Long after his fate was known;

Some said that nothing happened at all;
But even then, in the citadels, the "rope of fate"

Tightened a millimeter, and there were sickening knots,
Felt in the dark and passed over briefly

In rumors that he was bound and gagged by his sons
Until his fate could be forgotten

And that someone had glimpsed Jocasta
In the afterlife, holding her rope;

But even then, for Apollo, stranded alone in the palace,
A chariot appeared before his eyes,

Turning up in the god's story as it creaked away from
The palace, wobbling away from Thebes,

Past the cliff, where Laius, knowing
That any conversation with the Sphinx

Was a brush with death,
Quickened his horses, though

Passing under her cliff he could hear
Her riddles,

" . . . If you acquire an aura, an oracle, a horror, a laurel
For Apollo as if an oracle were an inherited jewel

You could pick up, sighted, in your right hand
And put down, blinded,

In your left, and if a jewel is like a word
You ordinarily would conceal, and confer,

As a father confers a bloodline in a moment
And abandons it, or extinguishes it . . ."

But, deeper into the journey, Laius stopped,
As if held fast, as if he had traveled to the end

Of a measured-out length of chain
Whose infinitesimal, adamantine links—

Invisible otherwise—
Intermittently flashed in his eyes

As the chain unreeled from a creaking
Pulley in Thebes.

And, stalled in his crimson wooden cart,
He peered ahead, vexed,

At the narrow, sun-dazzled road
Where a pedestrian,

Double-striking and deadly-footed,
Raised his walking-stick and struck him

In the skull, too soon, too soon—
And Laius saw a word rise to the surface,

Then melt itself into a concussion
Churning in silence;

Then a glimpse of Zeus
Seated in solitude

In a chair of blinding-white, pure snow;
Then a faceful of gravel.

Gravel, that gives no clues
About the mountain it broke off from long ago.

☗

SIX

THE ALPHABET
ENTERS GREECE

But that was before
The first, tiny alphabet letter

Entered into Greece for the first time,
The letter *Iota*, ι,

Like a fragile, fever-laden mosquito
Struck motionless by the divinity;

Struck soundless in the heart
Of barren Greece, where the god touched the letter

Uneasily, awed. Then *Delta* appeared silently
In the midst of the words, Δ,

Like the indelible mountain
With an infant king abandoned on it;

And *Theta*, like a human infant's face
Crossed out, θ,

Before *Lambda* appeared like a lame man
Leaning on a stick, λ,

And *Omega*, like a shining rope
Lowered by Zeus into the midst of things

And tied, by human hands,
Into a noose, Ω,

Before the slain Sphinx of *Psi*, Ψ,
Before the rock throne of *Eta*, H,

The Greek letters arranged in the Sphinx-poetry
Of their meaningless order,

Reeling across the surface of a metal leaf
Sent to the god as a tribute, or expressing remorse,

From the people of Thebes
And left at the temple gate:

ΑΒΓΔΕΖΗΘΙΚΛΜΝΞΟΠΡΣΤΥΦΧΨΩ
Sphinx-poetry. Filings from the iron passions,

Magnetized, conjoined in words, held fast;
Exposing a force.

The god claps his hands,
Calling a temple scribe to him:

The god: *Who established the order of the letters?*
The scribe: (*Silence.*)

The alphabet, in which lay hidden
The tale of Oedipus, no longer gouged out

In the gods' language, illegible to humans,
But written in Greek: the continuum of sound

That once streamed from the god's lips,
And the question Oedipus once brought to the god,

Now broken off and shut into the silence
Of written-down words, trapping the god's hexameters

Together with folktales shepherds told about tyrants
And gossip from an even older age

Into ΟΙΔΙΠΟΥΣ: the Greek letters,
Waiting in silence to be arranged

Into the comedies and tragedies,
Waiting to turn the people into gods

Who gaze at *things* tied
Into sequences of knots they can't undo,

Things to discuss, brood on, or quarrel over,
Helpless as gods to intervene;

The god touches the letters, one by one,
Arranging them in different ways,

Trying to find the orphan's real name,
Not the foundling's name used by slaves

And conferred by the queen in Corinth
As a title for his defect, "Swollen Foot,"

But the name the gods call him,
For the gods are known to call

People, places, things, and other gods
By their true names—

But there is no other name the god can find:
Only *Oedipus*, the letters shivering in the cold,

And a recurring phrase: "My-name-cringes-from-me"
Like an epithet, with a gust of archaic notes

Lifting the letters and showing nothing beneath,
A shepherd's music never written down,

Flute notes beyond the bourn of right and wrong,
Music that, once taken up, can't be put down—

Like the oracle Oedipus receives
And holds fast, turning away from the temple

To retreat back down the mountain
With his frightening answer,

Fleeing the god, fleeing his fate,
Fleeing his future crimes

On the throne of Corinth;
The god calls him back, too late, too late;

He hurries through the mountain paths,
Through gravel, in which everyone's footprints

Are clubfooted, even the god's—
He hurries toward Thebes, past ruined towns

Where perpetual wars are visible across
A countryside where everything is wrong,

The arson-blackened palaces, the empty slopes
Where mortals and the gods lay dead,

The temples plundered, the lyres broken;
Past the rubble-gates of Thebes and its broken stairs

To claim, with his answered riddle, the throne
That was his all along—

The god, on behalf of Zeus,
Calls *Oedipus! Oedipus!*

The only name he has to call him by.
Then strains to hear a reply.

He leans forward in his shining chair
In Delphi;

Nothing. Far up, he sees
His father's empty throne of snow,

And Olympus, dripping silence; silence; silence.
As if there is nothing that Zeus wants.

Oedipus! Oedipus! Nothing.
Yet Oedipus has heard the god;

And, seated on a throne of rock
In a shadowy wood, he lifts

His bandaged face in response.
Riddleless. Answerless.

SEVEN

✦

THE RIDDLE
IN REVERSE

In Delphi, the Sphinx reverses her riddle:
What is man?

What is—visible to all, but uninterpretable,
Like a Mycenaean beast engraved on a gem,

Animal, mortal, footed, biped, wingless,
Bringing a basket overflowing with offerings

Of scrolls and tablets
To a masked divinity seated on a throne,

Perhaps an emissary of Necessity
Bringing, with a panicked face, the news

That everything is true—a gem
Engraved in the royal workshops at the foot of the palace,

Whose image we can press in sealing wax
To make an immaculate replica in reverse

As fresh now as when it was presented
To the tyrant, without being able to say *what it is*—

What is man? The god calls the scribe
To him, and the scribe brings the god the Oedipus text

Laying the scroll in tribute at his feet:
A making known—the god touches it wonderingly

And, as he touches it, already the god's
Music glints in the Sophocles text.

And, as he touches it, the scribe of ice-crowned Necessity
Leans over the god's shoulder

And writes, in Greek letters,
Drive him away. The second oracle to Oedipus.

        = *the murderer of Laius*

ΕΛΑΥΝΕΤΕ
The Greek letters shiver in their graves;

At once, the god's voice
Passes through the words,

Passes through the worlds; Creon
Turns away, goes back down the mountain

While, in the far distance, on a more jagged mountain
The god of slaughter is blinded

And driven off—an enigmatic horror story
In the deep background,

Though in the god's telling this would never be explained,
Would be alluded to only once

And alluded to only in music, because music blunts
The cruelty of the text—

And once written down,
The oracle fuses into past and future,

Scribbled in tablets of dirtied wax,
Incised in Theban mud and Mycenaean clay,

And carved in human bone in the shepherds' fields,
And written by the paths worms make in excrement—

And engraved in miniature, undulating hexameters
In gold leaf so thin it shivers on the palm:

The god plucks a gold leaf from the basket
Of oracles in the temple and reads *Drive him away*—

Then crumples it into gold foil
And lets it fall from his hand for a slave's

Broom to sweep away. But his glimmering hexameters
Float visibly in the legend of Oedipus,

Bobbing in the breathing waves of the poetry
As if in the distant, shining fountain

Outside Thebes where Oedipus
Bathed his bloodied feet, the prophetic

Hexameters breaking over the maimed feet
In illegible waves. In Thebes, Oedipus

Receives Creon's message from the god
And answers: *Lock your doors against him,*

And the god sees, spilling from Oedipus' oracle,
An *eidolon*, a Greek ghost,

A figure staring ahead, blind and nameless,
A bringer of plague, a parricide, whose scars

His parents gave him as his name.
In all his life the god had never seen

Such a one: a shadow hanging on a blind man's crutch,
Called by the gods King Such-and-Such,

Called by himself the Know-Nothing—
A world-wonder, who spilled his sight away,

A flesh-and-blood monument to blood ties,
But a spectre excluded by magnitudes

The god cannot calculate,
The maimed feet still moving

Among the disjointed oracles, the maimed face
Surrounded by innumerable solitudes.

Then the Know-Nothing stops, listening,
Arrested in wonder, sifting his memory

For a slur or a blunder or a scar or a lie
Uneasily told, in a fleeting depression

He can't put his finger on: and a question
He goads himself to remember to bring

To the god: *Who could have been so pitiless,*
Who could have hurt this infant—

A dizzying event he can't envision,
Like a dream even the god can't interpret—

Some horrible event has been forgotten,
Some horrible solitude lies in the past,

Or lies in store, or lies in plain view, like a scar;
He can't remember what. The lyre, susceptible

To the god's mood, shivers with the malice
Of it, shakes off a savage dissonance

And goes dumb, sickened at the way
The human ones blunder so heavily into their graves

As Jocasta's rope is cut with a savage sawing-down
In the heart of the palace—

And Eyeless Necessity tugs, almost imperceptibly,
On a lyre string, tightening it

An immeasurably tiny distance until it snaps.
The god absently touches a broken string

Dangling from the lyre frame,
Then pulls it taut and swiftly refastens it.

But for the god of healing, helpless before the sight
Portrayed in the Sophocles scrolls,

For the god the black bolts
Of lightning have already fallen

In the shapes of Greek letters
And Zeus's scarlet rain covers

An actor's mask in Athens;
The musicians have been hired;

The actors have gathered around
A rehearsal lyre trembling with the god's notes;

The god is suddenly transfixed, as if seeing,
In the deep wilderness behind the stage,

Himself, with an infant in his arms, turning away;
Divinity, merely a background motif;

Tyranny, merely a background motif;
The chain of mountains, cresting with Olympus,

Diminutive, engraved on a gem embedded in a gold leaf
Locked in a royal box in the heart

Of the palace, where a father
Crosses a threshold; a son crosses it;

Everything is true;
The god of healing crouches on his throne.

EIGHT

✦

THE RUTHLESS
JEWEL

In the temple's inner room, there is a cloth suspended
From the lyre's high peak,

Embroidered with an illegible insignia
In crimson thread.

And the god's face hidden behind the cloth,
His left hand hangs in the wrist-strap

Of the instrument, limp, trapped,
As if it had hanged itself;

His right hand is suspended in a gesture
Like a Mycenaean king in crippled flight

Discovering a suicide
In his palace; but this is merely the gesture

Of the hand at the strings
As music is being made.

While, on a more remote mountainside, stranded in the future,
A rhapsode is telling a story

In which Sophocles
Is the Sphinx,

And Apollo is the pitying slave,
And Oedipus is a sacrifice—

But from whom to what?
From what to whom?

The god's face
Is a gray windblown room which no one enters

And no one answers the door
Though the heart pounds and pounds—

Eyeless Oedipus, without his mask,
Pounding at the temple's bronze door,

His cries reach the god:
That meddling shepherd lied,

I hate the man who saved me, I should have died.
But the god doesn't answer.

Oedipus hesitates,
Then turns, and slowly makes his way back down

The Sacred Way on his damaged feet,
Among the sacred statues he cannot see.

He walks as bent over as if he had strapped
A heavy throne to his back,

Having exchanged the first throne of Thebes
For a second throne of Corinth for a third

Throne of Thebes for a fourth, last,
Nameless, placeless, invisible throne—

A throne he means
To carry to the heart of things,

To set it down, to clamber onto it, and,
With bandaged eyes, to sit in judgment on himself.

And hidden but always glinting in Delphi's
Shadowy inmost room,

The most secret facet of the most ruthless jewel
Ever given to the god: the gods are born and die;

The gods are born in the same purple room
As slaves are born, and tyrants.

And the citizens of Thebes.
And the children of the gods.

There is no refuge for what-is-born,
Humans or gods.

It was too late, before this chain of worlds began.
Always too late. When a human is conceived

Far, far in the distance there appear
The figures of shovelers,

The dark ages spill from their shovels,
And a broken tablet with a fragment of the god's name.

The god can see the gods lying like the unburied dead
In the future's remote snows.

Then humans and the gods are shoveled under
The mountainside.

And the god cannot fashion a human life—
Except as humans do.

The god too has a child,
Above whose silken head at birth

The shovel appears. The god too has a fate.
The god too would intervene

Too late, too late—
The god of healing is helpless before these things.

Things; *things* he cannot save. When he touches
The strings the words form in the air:

What are such things, that even the gods can't repair?
What are the gods, who can't repair such things?

But because he is a god,
Nothing is said.

Because he is a god,
Birds fly in hushed circles near his head.

Lying far below the god's feet,
Old Thebes, a lightless trapezoid

Far in the future, fused into the heart of Greece,
Enigmatic, gone cold, turned in on itself,

The palace ceiling torn off
Where the rope was cut down,

And a hole torn in a mourning cloth
Draped over the empty throne of Labdacus

With *fate howling out of nowhere*;
And, farther up, the god's music,

A rending
Through which Zeus's golden rope hangs.

NINE

♛

A FLUTE
CARVED FROM
A BONE

And in the background, the slave who saved Oedipus
Waters the laurel—

The nameless slave, born into the household of Laius,
Who disobeyed the king,

Once a flute-playing shepherd assigned to slopes
Distant from Thebes, and now, in the language of the tablets,

"A servant of the god." A shepherd, nameless
Even in the gods' language,

Though the god has ransacked the tablets for his name,
But where the name should be

There is only a gouge in clay,
And when the god tries to call him

The god is struck mute,
Mouthing something uninterpretable,

As in the worlds-old dream in which
One can't speak out loud—

The god of poetry claps his hands instead
To call the shepherd to him,

And the shepherd appears, and crouches,
Covering his hair with his hands,

Expecting the god to pelt him with rebuke,
Holding out his arms

As if he stood beneath the overhanging roof
Of Laius, receiving again the nameless infant

Together with his atrocious orders,
While the eaves of the house of Labdacus

Tinkled above his head with icicles
From Olympus, dripping down his neck.

He waits for the god to pelt him with words,
With Sphinx-talk: *You should have died up there*—

He waits for the god to speak in wing beats,
Paraphrasing Oedipus; taking his part.

Outside, where Oedipus had stood pounding
At the bronze door with his question, there is only

A shivering void. The shepherd waits,
But nothing is said. He raises his face.

A moon comes and goes above Delphi,
Blue-tinted, scarred, a blind plague-face

Beneath which the god and the shepherd hear the faint,
Distant voices of children playing at

Lame Man, taking turns stumping forward with a stick
Near the abandoned palace: *You be Antigone*;

Bullies pushing them along, faintly singing little taunts,
Hobbledehoy, hobbledehoy,

And the god is mouthing words, but not in Greek.
That meddling shepherd lied.

Far above the citadel of Thebes
Time-scales seesaw, seesaw.

Oedipus' words come and go: *I should have died.*
Generations veer. Collide.

Then the slave, to avoid speaking, raises his flute
To his lips,

Enrapturing the god,
Enslaving him with the sound

Of a flute he carved from a bone
In the fields of Mount Kithairon,

Where long ago he played
As if there were no one else in the universe;

Even now, with his eyes closed,
He forgets the mute god,

As a slowly blown-out note softly
Drifts forward, like a feather from the Sphinx.

With the sound of a particle of sand
Crumbling from the Sphinx's face—

Beneath an icicle of sun
The god is rooted to the ground

The way he once stood ankle-deep
In the snows of Mount Olympus,

Oblivious to the cold, and what he saw
Could not be melted into Greek, something

That underlay the oracle:
Laius, don't have a child;

Something still tugging at the lyre,
Grown so heavy it nearly tears from his hands,

But the god does not loosen his grip;
His grip only tightens, and he lip-reads

The Greek words as they form in the air
Before his eyes:

At the sight of the infant's gaze
I was riveted, chosen, beguiled.

I knew what the oracle said.
And I rescued the child.

Then the god moves his hand and sweeps the strings,
And a dark wing, suddenly unfolding,

Lifts inward, with fleeting poetry
Spoken in wing beats,

Wing beats flying, always farther back,
And farther back,

Past those souls ready to be born,
Those never to be born, and those born long ago,

Past broken hearts and throngs of anxious mortals
Crowded into long-extinguished households,

Past visions embedded in the eyes
Of those who heeded or ignored the oracles,

Shepherds, flutists, slaves, blood kin,
Jocasta sleeping with her buried face

And her orphan looking back at his own birth
Through sequences of other births,

Looking ahead to his own death
Through sequences of other deaths,

And finally, at the most remote end
Of the guttering-out of a bloodline,

And at its beginning, the god sees
Himself, briefly rooted to the shining ground

= the nameless
slave ?

And holding the infant in its shroud
In the shining snows

Above the stage where the vexed words
Blindly rampage:

How can I forget with clues like these in my hands?
With the secret of my birth

Staring me in the face?
Then the god, touching the strings

With a gesture of flight,
Turns away from what happens below;

Rapt in unfolding insights
About snow——

Not justice, not law, not destiny,
Not sacrilege, not consequence,

Not causes and effects,
Not oracles——

But rapt in a glimmering cascade,
A barely audible arpeggio.

TEN

♛

THE PREMIERE
OF OEDIPUS

As, on a stage as bare as Greece,
A gong shatters the rocky slopes

Of the theater of Dionysus,
A gong of silence, like a concussion

Struck by the god, following upon the news
That the child was saved:

A gong, not a wing beat, of silence;
The loudest gong in barren Greece,

Audible for several miles; an abrupt stroke,
Struck with a goad

As if the god had struck Laius' skull,
Turning the wind red.

On Delphi, a flute's frail piping tries to follow along
With a fluttering, leaping upward

Of trills at first barely discerned
That shatter into grace notes,

But then the flute player clamps his fingertips
Over the finger holes to shut the sound away—

A silence trailed by a little, perplexed aftermath
Of unwelcome puns shuddering among

The god's distant strings, and a percussive,
Scourging rhythm, and the melting howls backstage—

All scrubbed away
By an angry, airborne silence,

As *Enter from the palace a messenger*
To report the name the tyrant called himself *know nothing*

In the heart of the palace—
A word the Greeks won't say, a word

That implicates the onlookers
Simply by being heard—

And summons into Greece a sequence
Of silences; the first silence

Overlaying the second;
The second, the third;

And the chorus, now finished for good
With veering from derision

To consolation and back again
In the blink of an eye—

The chorus wade three-deep into the silence,
Holding their hands over their mouths;

And the spectators on the hillside benches
Have pressed their fingers in their ears,

As if this were not silence, but deafness;
As if they all were afraid

That the word, rising up,
Could make their ears bleed—

Ill-starred man, may you never know
Who you are.

Then a housefly falling down
From a ziggurat of housefly ancestors

Alights on stage and shakes its fist,
Raising a wail that climbs

So high it falls down between
Two shivers of sound,

Instantly silenced.
A diminutive wail that, cut off, seems in its absence

To have been monstrous. A wail riveting the god
Of poetry to his shining chair

In the universe above Thebes.
Then rivulets of wails appear in Greek, at once

Extinguished by the god, as if the pulsing star
By which Oedipus navigated

From Delphi into Thebes had been extinguished
By a sack of pouring sand.

Still, it is impossible, even for the god of music,
To create a silence that cannot be broken.

A sound will seep through.
It can't be shut away.

At the heart of the music,
A slamming silence in the heart of Greece.

At the heart of the slamming silence,
A wobbling cart appears in the far distance,

A royal chariot that stalls at the crossroads
Lying in the far-flung loneliness

Between the heights of Kastri and Bardana.
Laius, coming to visit the god,

Coming to ask the god about the fate
Of the three-day-old he set aside.

But the god has turned away,
And moves his hand.

The god moves his hand; perhaps surrendering:
Let what comes next, come next,

His task is to wield, to brandish a note
That assails the layers of stunned silence

At the heart of the text;
To register cataclysm in a single pitch;

To give his music over to qualms
Of a sort the gods gaze in awe at; he touches a string;

Even Ares, who abhors music, stops frantically pounding
On the Theban's doors; even Zeus,

Stricken, looks up; a pang,
A tremor registering in waves

That reverberate beneath his hand,
The like of which even the god of music

Has never heard before.
He touches a string with the sound

The earth makes as it brushes past the air:
A sound that soft.

With the sound a feather makes, aloft
And hurling itself from here to there.

Then he stops the string with the sound of a fingertip
Closing forever an infant's eyes—

In the white-and-purple mountain's
Untouched snows

The god has turned from gazing
Over many-roofed, shining Delphi,

Past bare gray slopes, ravines,
And tortured trees,

At a horse-drawn cart that travels toward him
From the citadel of Thebes:

An irritable king, impetuous, vexed,
Accompanied by an entourage of four,

Led by his emissary to the oracle: the herald
With his wand, sacrilege to assault.

Five men approach the god on the narrow road
That twists into the heart

Of brilliant Greece.
Behind the king, concealed

By a local mountain range,
His embedded palace gleams

In Thebes like a ruthless jewel
In a seal-ring passed down and down;

Ahead, the god's glittering shrine
Is blinding on the mountain.

He shades his eyes, a royal figure traveling
On an affair of state to the god

With offerings to ask the oracle:
What was the infant's fate?

He leans from his crimson cart
To strike with his goad a man on foot

Who obstructs his urgent passage to the god,
And comes to a halt,

With a tiny *skreak* of the wooden wheels,
Like a housefly's wail,

Like the squeak of the pegs rotating
In their holes:

Far up in the glinting, undefiled
Cleft of Delphi, music is being made

By the god, who turns from the sight
And closes his eyes—

I was riveted, chosen, beguiled—
The god who, delicately,

As if plucking a single fate
From a heap of entangled fates,

Touches a string and replies:
I rescued the child.

NOTES

The Throne of Labdacus is rooted in Greek legend, myth, history, drama, and religion, and the reader may be helped by the following notes.

Labdacus was the grandfather of Oedipus and the father of Laius.

The legend of Oedipus existed in many versions, and was well known to Sophocles' audience. In Sophocles' version, Laius, the childless king of Thebes, seeks the advice of the Delphic oracle about what he must do to have a child; the oracle answers indirectly that he will die at the hands of his son. He and his wife, Jocasta, nonetheless conceive and give birth to a son. Fearing the oracle, they pierce his ankles with an iron pin when he is three days old and give him to a household slave with orders to expose him in the wilderness. Overcome with pity, the slave gives the baby to a shepherd, who brings him to Polybus and Merope, the childless king and queen of Corinth. They name the boy Oedipus ("Swollen Foot") after his injured feet. When Prince Oedipus is about eighteen, he is taunted by a drunk who tells him that he is not the true child of Polybus and Merope. Although they insist he is their child, Oedipus is disturbed; he travels to Delphi to ask Apollo who his parents are. Apollo does not answer his question directly, but reveals to Oedipus that he will kill his father and marry his mother. Horrified, Oedipus rushes away from Delphi, in a direction opposite to Corinth, vowing never to return there. About twelve miles from Delphi, he encounters an older man—Laius—who imperiously orders him to get out of the way and strikes at him in the narrow road. Oedipus kills the man and his entourage. He continues his journey, encountering as he approaches the city of Thebes the riddling Sphinx, who has been killing the young men of Thebes when they cannot answer her riddle: What goes on four legs in the morning, two at noon, and three in the evening? Oedipus answers her riddle correctly with the word "Man"; she is vanquished, and she kills herself. When Oedipus arrives in Thebes, the city learns that he has brought the Sphinx's reign of terror to an end, and out of gratitude to him, the city, which has recently lost its king, awards him the throne of Thebes and the hand of the Theban queen, Jocasta, in marriage. They have four children together. Many years later, a plague ravages Thebes, and as the Sophocles drama opens, Oedipus sends a delegation to Delphi to ask the oracle what is causing the plague. Again indirectly, the oracle replies that the murderer of Laius is in Thebes and must be found and driven out, and Oedipus undertakes to discover who the murderer is.

The Greek gods spoke their own language among themselves, rather than Greek, and their language was mostly unknown to humans. The Greek alphabet was known to the ancient Greeks to be a human invention, derived from Phoenician letters, and Greek was considered to be a human language (in contrast to the belief in ancient Israel that the Hebrew alphabet was God-given and that Hebrew was God's language). The legendary attribution of the invention of the Greek alphabet to the city of Thebes and to Cadmus, its Phoenician founder, has not been borne out by modern scholarship. That Thebes had numerous ties to the Near East (Phoenicia, Persia, Assyria, and Babylonia) is not disputed. Artefacts of Babylonian cuneiform writing were discovered in the burned remains of the first Theban palace and are now on display in the museum at Thebes.

The stuff of Greek religion is the myths, communicated in poetry; the myths are not dogmatic, but are mutable and multivalent, sculpted in water rather than carved in stone. Each myth retains a core identity even as it takes on an individual poet's unique stamp and seal.

In Greek belief, the Olympian gods did not create the world, and a god such as Apollo was not the source of human life, except occasionally as a parent, with mortals, of mortals. The gods were not philosophers, they were not historians of divine or human affairs, and they did not give explanations, in revelation, of how or why the world came to be. They issued very little in laws, commands, or codes of behavior. The gods were innumerable, and much about them remained mysterious and fugitive; but we do know that the gods, with the possible exception of Zeus, were fallible, fate-bound (even Zeus is bound to honor fate in the *Iliad*: XVI), vulnerable to becoming attached to humans, and, it is subtly suggested, subject to necessity. Oracles were crucial in Greek religion, but difficult for humans to heed because often they were brilliantly double-edged, oblique, or ambiguous. In the Sophocles *Oedipus* the oracles are inescapable and not open to amelioration through (even free) human choice or action: Oedipus' choices are immaterial.

All the ancient poets agree that the gods involved themselves in the stories of human existence, at least as passionately curious spectators or as commentors, when they did not actively intervene; and, most consequentially for humans, they involved themselves as lovers (or as rapists) of humans, whose every sexual encounter with them would result in the birth of a child. The gods' human descendants were mortal, and the gods, even Zeus, suffered over the deaths of their mortal children. But their attachments to humans were volatile, and they could as soon be moved to pity as they could turn away from the sight of human tragedy with divine indifference. There is an implication in the myths that in the end the gods would always turn away from the humans they cared about, perhaps because humans were heading into death and the gods were not.

The Zeus of Sophocles' *Oedipus Tyrannus* differs from the Homeric Zeus (whose identity as an idling playboy has been somewhat exaggerated in popular reputation). The Sophoclean Zeus is invisible, remote, all-knowing, the giver of law; he is pervasive and unfailing, and his intentions are unknowable. What happens, happens because Zeus has willed it to happen; as the god of prophecy, Apollo speaks for Zeus, his father. Apollo does not cause what his prophecies describe, and he never elaborates upon or explains his oracles. Because Apollo's oracle to Oedipus does not mention the self-blinding or state that in the future Oedipus will ruinously seek out his identity, it often is assumed, in discussions of the tragedy, that these acts of Oedipus must therefore lie outside the design of fate-bound actions. More curiously, Oedipus' claim that his self-blinding is his own work, not Apollo's, is generally taken at face value. But we cannot know if this claim is correct (Oedipus is not all-knowing, and throughout his life he has mistaken many things both human and divine), nor can we assume that Zeus did not plan and that Apollo did not foresee that Oedipus should undertake to discover the truth of his life (after all, *Know thyself* is a Delphic prescription, written on the wall of Apollo's temple at Delphi). We can say for certain that the gods do not disclose everything and are under no compulsion to do so; and we know, furthermore, that we and Oedipus still do not know everything at the tragedy's end. In the Greek religious view, fate and free will need not be paradoxical or opposed (Heraclitus observes that character is fate). Tiresias prophesies the blindness of Oedipus, and therefore the self-blinding, although a chosen and free act, could be fate-bound as well. We cannot know. And the gods do not say.

Some of the italicized lines and phrases in this poem are from *Oedipus Tyrannus*, which I have taken or adapted from various translations:

Polybus has taken . . . (p. 25): Translated by Bernard Knox in *Oedipus at Thebes* (New Haven: Yale University Press, 1957).

Ill-starred man . . . (pp. 30 and 87): Translated by Charles Segal in *Oedipus Tyrannus: Tragic Heroism and the Limits of Knowledge* (New York: Twayne Publishers, 1993).

Double-striking and deadly-footed (p. 45): Translated by David Seale in *Vision and Stagecraft in Sophocles* (London: Croom Helm, 1982).

The following are taken or adapted from the translation of Stephen Berg and Diskin Clay in *Oedipus the King* (New York: Oxford University Press, 1978):

Whipping a storm (p. 28)
Drive him away (p. 59)

Lock your doors . . . (p. 60)
I hate the man . . . (p. 68)
fate howling . . . (p. 72)
I should have died . . . (p. 77)
How can I forget . . . (p. 81)

The following phrases are taken from these sources:
"black sack of trouble" (p. 25): Homer's *Odyssey*, XII.31, translated by Robert Fitzgerald (New York: Doubleday & Company, 1961).

A foot signifies a slave (p. 16): Adapted from Artemidorus, *Oneirocritica*, translated by Robert J. White (Park Ridge, N.J.: Noyes Press, 1975).

Animal, mortal, footed . . . (p. 57): Aristotle, *Posterior Analytics*, II.5 (New York: Random House, 1941): the answer Aristotle gives to his question "What is the essential nature of man?"

All other italicized or quoted phrases attributed in this poem to Zeus, Apollo, Necessity, the Sphinx, Oedipus, and the nameless slave are my invention. That Olympus is snowy and cold does not accord with the Homeric vision of a warm and radiantly sunny home for the gods on, or above, the mountaintop.

The law attributed to Apollo and Zeus on pp. 27–28 is my invention, although it is founded upon the assertion Zeus makes about the misery of men in the *Iliad*, XVII:446ff.

The oracle *Laius, don't have a child* is not identical to the oracle in Sophocles; I have stated it so that it falls between the conditional "if . . . then" oracle in Aeschylus and the unconditional prophecy to Laius, "Your son will . . . ," reported by Jocasta in Sophocles.

According to the messenger who comes out to report on the catastrophe inside the palace, Oedipus rushes inside and cries out for a sword, which apparently he is not given; he then breaks down the bedroom door and unties Jocasta's noose and lowers her body to the floor. In this poem, I have put the sword into the hand of Oedipus, in order to have him cut down Jocasta's rope rather than untying the knot. In Sophocles, when Oedipus describes the murder of Laius, he says at several different times that Laius was "cut down" at the crossroads. Oedipus has "cut down" both of his parents. In *Antigone* (lines 669–76), as translated by Robert Fagles (New York: Penguin, 1984), the Chorus says of this family:

some god will bring them crashing down . . .
in the house of Oedipus, the hope's cut down in turn
by the long, bloody knife swung by the god of death . . .

Although I have used the word "ghost" (p. 60), an *eidolon* is a phantom double, not a visitor from the afterlife.

Although I have referred to Oedipus as "the tyrant," he is not a tyrant in the modern sense. The Greek *tyrannus* is a usurper of the throne rather than a dictator. Oedipus, the native-born heir to the throne of Thebes, has returned as a foreigner and usurped the throne to which he was born.

The golden rope of Zeus is from the *Iliad*, VIII:18–27; the binding rope of fate is immemorial.

In Greek belief there existed Unwritten Laws, which were generated on Olympus (as the Chorus of *Oedipus* proclaims in the second stasimon). The Unwritten Laws are the true, deathless, and cosmic laws out of which human laws devolve.

The mortality of the gods is speculated upon by the Chorus in the second stasimon of *Oedipus Tyrannus*.

Apollo, in his aspect as Paieon, would receive offerings of hymns from the Greeks and could be won over by human music-making.